PICTORIAL
EDINBURGH
SERIES

EDINBURGH'S NEW TOWN
AND ITS ENVIRONS

PICTORIAL
EDINBURGH
SERIES

Malcolm Cant

EDINBURGH'S NEW TOWN
AND ITS ENVIRONS

To
the memory of
Charlie

Charles James Trotter
1934–1987
a close friend and loyal colleague

First published in 2009 by
Stenlake Publishing Ltd
54–58 Mill Square,
Catrine KA5 6RD
01290 551122
www.stenlake.co.uk

ISBN: 978-1-84033-472-2

British Library Cataloguing-in-Publication Data

A catalogue record for this book is available on request

Book and cover design by Mark Blackadder

Printed in China

CONTENTS ❧

BY THE SAME AUTHOR

Marchmont in Edinburgh 1984
Villages of Edinburgh Volume 1 (North) 1986
Villages of Edinburgh Volume 2 (South) 1987
Edinburgh: Sciennes and the Grange 1990
Yerbury: A Photographic Collection 1850-1993 1994
Edinburgh: Gorgie and Dalry 1995
Villages of Edinburgh: An Illustrated Guide Volume 1 (North) 1997
The District of Greenbank in Edinburgh 1998
Villages of Edinburgh: An Illustrated Guide Volume 2 (South) 1999
Old Tollcross, Morningside and Swanston 2001
Marchmont, Sciennes and the Grange 2001
Old Dalry in Edinburgh 2002
Old Gorgie 2002
Edinburgh from the Air: 70 Years of Aerial Photography 2003
Old Dean and Stockbridge 2004
Knowing Your Grandfather 2004
Edinburgh Shops Past and Present 2005
Edinburgh People at Work and Leisure 2006
South Edinburgh 2007
Edinburgh's Old Town and Its Environs 2008

INTRODUCTION AND ACKNOWLEDGEMENTS

Edinburgh's New Town and Its Environs is an obvious sequel to *Edinburgh's Old Town and Its Environs*, my previous book in the Pictorial Edinburgh Series.

Part 1 deals with Princes Street, beginning at the West End. As we prepare for Edinburgh's principal thoroughfare to be served by a new tramway system, it is pertinent to observe how previous transport systems evolved to meet the problems of the day.

Part 2 deals with Charlotte Square, George Street and St Andrew Square. The geometric layout of the First New Town is very evident in photographs from the 1950s where the absence of parked vehicles shows the streetscape to best advantage. There are also photographs of human interest including bankers, tradesmen and young men starting out on their careers in insurance.

The colour section is captioned 'Princes Street, Shops, Clocks and Interiors'. The display windows of Small's and Darling's in Princes Street are included and a wide range of public clocks in churches, hotels and public buildings. Other photographs include the interior of the Queen Street home of the Royal College of Physicians Edinburgh and the recently redesigned interior of St Paul's and St George's Church.

Part 3 is centred on the Western New Town beginning at Shandwick Place and going as far west as Donaldson's Hospital. The cathedrals, many of the churches, and several elegant crescents and terraces are photographed. This part also includes Queen Street and the area around Picardy Place and Broughton Street where the Theatre Royal once stood.

Part 4 deals with the northern and eastern parts of the New Town. It begins with St Paul's and St George's Episcopal Church in York Place and proceeds northwards to Broughton, Bellevue, Canonmills and Stockbridge. The eastern section includes a 1867 panoramic view from Calton Hill and a 1930s aerial view showing the Bridewell and Calton Jail in the course of demolition.

Many of the photographs in the book have been contributed by individuals whose names appear throughout the text. I am particularly indebted, again, to Barbara Simpson for allowing me to use pictures by her late father, Norward Inglis, and also Mrs Sheila Wilkie for the use of pictures by her late husband, John K. Wilkie. Another group of pictures, dated 1929, has been lent by Malcolm Wood. Yvonne Grant also provided excellent colour photographs of Small's and Darling's in Princes Street. The book is further enhanced by several modern photographs, particularly in the colour section, by my friend Phil Seale.

Alan Brotchie has provided photographs and information for my captions on public transport, and Douglas Glass has given equally detailed information on private transport. Robin Sherman also provided several pictures from his extensive Edinburgh collection, particularly the view of Princes Street which appears on the book cover. Many other people have been involved on individual subjects. In alphabetical order they are: George Baird; Colin Dale; Mrs Catherine Davidson; Hamish Davidson; Jimmy Hogg; John Knight; Ian Macaskill; Bruce McKain; Ian Milne; Anne Robinson; Mairi Simpson; Brian Smith; and Peter Stubbs.

The staff of several organisations have also assisted: the Church Army; Edinburgh City Archives; Edinburgh Room of the Central Library; Faculty of Advocates; Lee Boyd Architects; National Gallery of Scotland; National Museum of Scotland; Northern Lighthouse Board; Palmerston Place Church; Royal College of Physicians Edinburgh; Royal Scottish Academy of Art and Architecture; St Mary's Episcopal Church; St Mary's Roman Catholic Cathedral; St Paul's and St George's Episcopal Church; and the Scottish National Portrait Gallery.

As with all my previous books, I received assistance from a small group of professional people without whose commitment I would be unable to get the book ready for publication: Nicola Wood has done an excellent job editing the script; Mark Blackadder designed the book and the jacket to match the other books in the Pictorial Edinburgh Series; Oula Jones added a comprehensive index; and Richard Stenlake brought it all together for publication.

As always, I thank my wife, Phyllis, and the members of our extended family, including several grandchildren, for their interest and encouragement.

Malcolm Cant
2009

PART 1

WEST END

PRINCES STREET

MOUND

EAST END

Part 1 of *Edinburgh's New Town and Its Environs* is devoted, appropriately, to its principal thoroughfare, Princes Street. Although its position is really unrivalled in Edinburgh, it was George Street which was intended to be the centre of James Craig's plans for the New Town. Even the name, Princes Street, was a second choice. The first choice of name was St Giles Street but that was quickly abandoned because of its association with an unsavoury part of London by the same name. Princes Street was first laid out in the last quarter of the

eighteenth century as a series of three-storey terraced houses with basements. Several blocks still exist, including one basement which can be reached directly from the pavement, but most have been heavily overlaid by later developments. By the end of the nineteenth century, the hotels, department stores and insurance offices had supplanted many of the original houses, especially towards the east end of the street. At the present day, several gems remain, waiting to be rediscovered, but many more have been lost over the years.

The arrangement of photographs is topographical, starting at the West End and moving eastwards. There are several views of the main junction, including well-known shops such as Aitken & Niven, Maule's and Macvitties Guest. Princes Street has always been the principal route for ceremonial occasions from royal processions to more domestic parades organised annually by organisations such as the Boys' Brigade and the Boy Scouts. At the time of writing, the street has been closed to vehicular traffic for several months to allow the

❧ The undated photograph, by the well-known Edinburgh photographer, R. A. Rayner, of the West End of Edinburgh, is captioned 'Coronation Day, Edinburgh'. Edward VII was crowned on 9 August 1902 and George V on 22 June 1911. However, as Aitken & Niven, the clothiers, did not occupy the corner premises until 1905 the photograph must be dated 1911. *Malcolm Cant Collection.*

❧ The same scene is clearly much earlier at the time when the corner shops were occupied, from left to right, by: Caledonian Bazaar; James Drummond's latest novelties in gloves, hats and ties; and W. Vallance, the confectioner. The West End clock was moved to the junction of Leith Walk and London Road in the early 1960s. *Malcolm Cant Collection.*

construction of rails for the city's new tramway system. Several photographs are included, however, showing aspects of public and private transport over the years, none of them nearly so ambitious as that now under construction – or so we are led to believe. There are examples of coaches, horse trams and cable cars all with the top deck open to the weather. By the time of Edinburgh's first electric tramway system (1923–56) the travel experience was relatively comfortable.

Princes Street Gardens have also been included. The very earliest bandstand dates from 1877 and was replaced in 1935 but is still hopelessly inadequate for modern use. The Ross Bandstand and the Ross Fountain were both gifted to the city but not, as is popularly believed, by the same family. There is also a picture of the unveiling of the equestrian statue to the Royal Scots Greys in 1906.

The east end of Princes Street was the area first affected by the appearance of large commercial buildings in place of the terraced houses. Some very grand buildings were erected, notably the head offices of the Life Association of Scotland, near the Mound, and the North British & Mercantile Insurance Company on the site of present-day British Home Stores. The loss of those buildings has greatly reduced the architectural merit of the street.

The last few pages of Part 1 are given over

This traditional view of the West End, *c.* 1904, shows, on the left, the retail premises of Robert Maule & Son with their royal coat-of-arms on the corner above the window blinds. Robert Maule opened his first business in Kincardine in 1856 and moved to Tolbooth Wynd, in Leith, in 1872. He secured the prestigious Princes Street site in 1893, which became Binns in 1934, and later Frasers. *Malcolm Cant Collection.*

to the area from Waverley Bridge to the former General Post Office building at the East End. Already there is a significant proportion of the population who have no memories of the Waverley Market (now Princes Mall), as the venue for a wide variety of shows and exhibitions, including flower shows, Ideal Homes Exhibitions, circuses and carnivals. The photographs included are of the Civic Exhibition in 1963.

No collection of Princes Street photographs should be without a comparison between the Balmoral Hotel (opened as the North British Hotel) and the rather haphazard

collection of buildings which were on the site before 1902. Although the Balmoral is now seen as one of the jewels in the crown, its huge bulk was criticised when first built because of its impact on Register House immediately opposite. This section of the book is completed by three photographs relating to the General Post Office: the first is a traditional view of the building, looking, from the outside at any rate, very much as it does today; the second is a group of postmen in 1905; and the last is the most interesting of all – an illustration of the laying of the foundation stone on 23 October 1861.

In 1937 Edinburgh's public transport system was dominated by the electric tram which had been introduced in 1923 to replace the previous cable car system. The tram on the right of the picture is heading south on service No. 13 but the tram in the centre (at the Belisha beacon crossing) is not showing a route number. It is an 'extra', probably heading for the turning point in Princes Street opposite the Waverley Steps. Belisha beacon crossings, named after the politician, Leslie Hore-Belisha, were forerunners to Zebra and Pelican crossings. They had a constantly flashing light in an orange globe, mounted on a post, to assist pedestrians to cross the road. Castle Terrace is in the background with the Poole's Synod Hall (used as a picture house until 1965) in the position of present-day Saltire Court, and Moir & Baxter Ltd., automobile agents and engineers, on the corner with Lothian Road. The main entrance to the Caledonian Hotel is on the extreme right of the picture. When this picture was taken, the entrance to the Caledonian Station was immediately to the right of the hotel entrance. The small car passing the hotel is a 1929 Austin 7. *Malcolm Cant Collection.*

By the time of this photograph, the electric tram system had been phased out for some time (since 1956) and traffic lights had been installed along the entire length of Princes Street. The traffic arrangement is not dissimilar to what it was in 2009 immediately before the introduction of Edinburgh's latest tramway system. To the east of the junction with South Charlotte Street, private cars are parked along the line of what is now a wider pavement on the shops' side of the street. *Photograph by John K. Wilkie.*

❧ *Above left*. On the right, an open-topped cable car is travelling south on Lothian Road. On Princes Street, the name 'Macvitties Guest' appears on the face of the tallest building with the triangular-shaped top storey. The lower building to the right of it (on the corner of South Charlotte Street) was demolished in 1924 for an extension to Macvitties (see pages 8 & 9). *Malcolm Cant Collection.*

❧ *Below left*. In this early view of St John's Episcopal Church, designed by William Burn in 1815, the terrace and undercroft on the south side are more visible than they are at the present day owing to the absence of vegetation. *Courtesy of Robin Sherman.*

❧ *Above right*. A very substantial triumphal arch was erected across the west end of Princes Street for the royal visit to Edinburgh in 1911 of George V following his accession to the throne on 6 May 1910. The picture shows the Yeomanry escort under the archway. *Malcolm Cant Collection.*

❧ *Below right*. This unusual view is taken from St John's Episcopal Church, looking west across the bottom of Lothian Road towards Rutland Street that can be seen on the right. The Caledonian Railway Princes Street Station, with the clock, was replaced by a much more substantial building in 1893 which was extended upwards a decade later to include the present-day Caledonian Hotel. *Malcolm Cant Collection.*

❧ *Above left*. On the left of the picture, the horse car going to Leith is easily overtaking the heavily loaded coach, *Dalmeny*, which has 'Forth Bridge & Queensferry' on the tailboard. The sign for the Central Hotel at No. 121 Princes Street can be seen on the chimney stack. *Courtesy of A. W. Brotchie.*

❧ *Below left*. This early 1930s view shows that the public transport system is clearly the electric tram, with 'island' stops, at intervals, along the length of Princes Street. The shop blind on the left says 'Maules' which became Binns in 1934. On the right there is an electric tram which has been converted from an open-topped cable car. *Malcolm Cant Collection.*

❧ *Above right*. By 1920 the same section of roadway is very much more congested, but at least these cable cars have been fitted with the luxury of covers for top-deck passengers. The advertisement on the side of the nearest cable car is for Jas. Thomson & Sons of No. 5 Leven Street, purveyors of Edinburgh oatmeal. The policeman on points duty has not yet been alerted to the predicament of the lady with the pram. *Courtesy of A. W. Brotchie.*

❧ *Below right*. Edinburgh's first electric tram system came to an end in 1956. A few years later, the increase in private cars is evident but, surprisingly, there are not all that many buses. *Malcolm Cant Collection.*

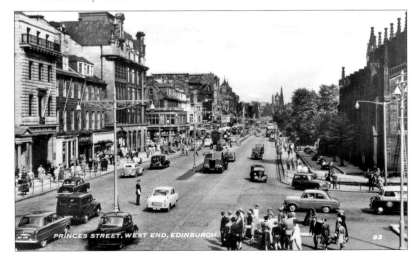

In this 1950s photograph the car turning left off Princes Street is a 1950 Bentley with a Park Ward drophead coupe body. The building on the corner (also seen on the opposite page) is occupied by Macvitties, Guest & Co. Ltd., bakers and confectioners. The firm is believed to have been founded in Queensferry Street in 1830 by William Thomson, a member of the Incorporation of Baxters (or bakers) in the Dean village nearby. Thomson's business was bought in 1837 by Robert Macvittie, whose descendants went into partnership with Edward Graham Guest in 1898. The building was erected in three separate stages with different, but complementary, styles of architecture. The first stage, in 1903, was L-shaped, with tall narrow frontages to Princes Street and South Charlotte Street, built around an existing house on the corner. In the photograph the Princes Street frontage is marked by vertical drapes above ground floor level.
Malcolm Cant Collection.

The second stage of development was in 1924 when the corner house was bought and replaced by a substantial building joining the two 1903 narrow frontages to Princes Street and South Charlotte Street. The third, and last, stage, containing the popular function suite, the Charlotte Rooms, was by the architects, Cairns & Ford, in 1935, after this photograph was taken. In this 1929 photograph, the intended third stage site, immediately south of Hope Street Lane, is still occupied by the original three-storey tenement with the addition of a shop front for John Wilson & Son, Irish linen merchants. Delivery vans are parked outside the South Charlotte Street frontage of the first stage. The van nearest to the camera is fitted with a roof rack in which the empty biscuit tins were stacked after collection from retail outlets. The second van is a Citroen and the third, a Trojan. *Courtesy of Malcolm Wood.*

✤ *Below right.* The original bandstand in West Princes Street Gardens was a fairly modest structure, erected in 1877 at a cost of £500. In 1964, a photograph, not unlike this one, was sent to the *Edinburgh Evening News & Dispatch* by an amateur photographer, Thomas Conston of Morningside Road. Mr Conston had taken the photograph on 23 April 1924 when 20,000 people packed into the gardens to hear the city's first wireless message – King George V's speech from Wembley. *Courtesy of Betty Cuthill.*

✤ *Below.* As can be seen from this photograph, the bandstand became a very popular venue offering a wide variety of music by both military and civilian bands. *Malcolm Cant Collection.*

✤ *Right.* When the old bandstand had outlived its usefulness, it was replaced by a stone-built structure with a raised terrace for seating. Despite small extensions in the past it has become hopelessly inadequate for the type of shows now attracted to the Gardens. It was opened on Friday 10 May 1935 as a gift to the city from William Henry Ross, chairman of Distillers Company Ltd., to mark the Silver Jubilee of King George V. *Malcolm Cant Collection.*

Band in Princes St. Gardens, Edinburgh

Left. The Ross Fountain, in West Princes Street Gardens, was cast in iron by A. Durenne of Paris for the International Exhibition of 1862. It was purchased by the Edinburgh gunsmith, Daniel Ross, and gifted to the city, but, initially, it was not greeted with universal approval. *Courtesy of Robin Sherman.*

Below left. To the left of the flight of steps leading to the Mound is the statue, in Carrara marble, of Allan Ramsay by Sir John Steell. Ramsay, born in 1686 in Leadhills, Lanarkshire, led a very industrious life as a bookseller and writer of many songs and poems. Latterly, he lived in the octagonal-shaped house in Ramsay Garden at the head of Castlehill. *Photograph by Norward Inglis.*

Below. Edinburgh's Floral Clock, the first of its kind in Britain, began ticking on 10 June 1903. Initially it had an hour hand only, the minute hand being added in 1904. It was built by James Ritchie & Son of Edinburgh. The photograph shows the 1953 design for the coronation of Elizabeth II. *Photograph by Duncan McMillan.*

The Boys' Brigade was founded by William Smith in Glasgow in 1883. At the founder's day parade in Edinburgh in 1957 the guard of honour was provided by the 55th company attached to St Matthew's Parish Church in Morningside. *Front rank, left to right*: Sgt. George Adams; John Watson; Hendry Girdwood; Robert Muat; Alex MacKay; Sinclair Finlay; Michael Davidson; Charles Haggie; Charles Barnes; Ernest Chalmers; Edward Over. *Second rank, left to right*: George Urquhart; Laurence Goudie; James Logan; Drew McLaughlan; James Downie. *Officers at the rear*: Lt. Phil Montador; Staff Sgt. William Meek; Lt. Alec McLaren; Lt. Dave Dickson. *Courtesy of Robert Muat.*

Left. On what looks like a typical winter's day in Edinburgh, a large crowd has gathered for the unveiling ceremony on 16 November 1906 of the memorial to the members of the Royal Scots Greys who died in the Boer War (1899–1902). In the conflict the regiment lost seven officers, sixty-seven men and thousands of horses. The memorial in West Princes Street Gardens was sculpted by W. Birnie Rhind and unveiled by the Earl of Rosebery. The regiment can trace its history to 1678 when Lt.-General Tam Dalyell raised a force to suppress the Covenanters. In 1971 the Royal Scots Greys united with the 3rd Carabiniers to form the Royal Scots Dragoon Guards, Scotland's only regular cavalry regiment which now forms part of the Royal Armoured Corps. *Malcolm Cant Collection.*

Below. Almost fifty years after the unveiling of the memorial, the Edinburgh skyline is unaltered. The cars, from left to right, are: Morris Cowley, produced 1954–56; Morris Minor, Series II version, produced 1954–56, the registration RM denoting Cumberland County Council; Hillman Minx, Mark VI version, produced 1953–54; and Standard Vanguard, Phase II version, produced 1953–55. *Malcolm Cant Collection.*

Right. Darling's at No. 124 Princes Street, with the exterior of the building decorated for the coronation of King Edward VII in 1902. The shop to the left is Scott Brothers, linen merchants, at No. 125, and the shop to the right, Allan's, the bootmakers. *Courtesy of Robert Murray Stamp Shop.*

Below. In 1959 the autumn window display at Small's at No. 106 Princes Street was by Sandy Davidson. By that time, fibre glass models (with heads) were beginning to replace the much heavier models, without heads. *Courtesy of Mrs Catherine Davidson.*

Far right. In the early 1960s, a very 'modern' window display on the theme 'Optic Art', was arranged by Sandy Davidson at Jaeger, No. 119A Princes Street. *Courtesy of Mrs Catherine Davidson.*

❧ *Top left.* Princes Street, *c.* 1910, looking east, with two open-topped cable cars in the distance. Car No. 54, on service No. 5 (on the right of the picture) is a cable car which was constructed with a top-deck covered roof that greatly improved the comfort of the upper deck passengers. Electric light has been installed in the pavement lamp standards but the light on the central island looks like an early gas fitting (later converted to electricity). The sign, high up on the lamp standard implores Edinburgh's citizens to maintain high standards of hygiene: PLEASE DO NOT SPIT ON THE PAVEMENT. *Malcolm Cant Collection.*

❧ *Centre left.* About two decades later, Princes Street has been transformed, with central electric light and overhead lines to provide power to the electric tram system, introduced in 1923. The same system of central islands is in use, and already there are several private cars parked on both sides of the street. *Courtesy of Alex Seggar.*

❧ *Lower left.* This unusual, undated photograph shows a solitary pedestrian walking towards the rear elevation of the Royal Scottish Academy (now the Royal Scottish Academy Building). *Malcolm Cant Collection.*

❧ *Below.* At the entrance to the Royal Scottish Academy there is much more action during the royal visit to Edinburgh of Queen Mary. She became queen when her husband George V acceded to the throne on 6 May 1910. She died in 1953. *Malcolm Cant Collection.*

Right. In 1809 the North British Insurance Company was established in a small office in what is now Parliament Square. In 1812 the company moved to the corner of Bank Street and the Lawnmarket, and then to No. 1 Hanover Street in 1825. It was not until 1842 that the company bought a house at No. 64 Princes Street which was demolished for the construction of a prestigious building suitable as a head office. This is the building with doorways at Nos. 64 and 65 on the right of the picture. *From* North British & Mercantile Insurance Company 1809–1909. *Courtesy of May Hoy.*

Below. During the second half of the nineteenth century, the company established branches throughout the United Kingdom and abroad, and became the North British & Mercantile Insurance Company in 1862. At the beginning of the twentieth century a completely new head office was built at Nos. 64 and 65 which was demolished in the 1960s and replaced by the vastly inferior architecture of British Home Stores. *Courtesy of May Hoy.*

Below right. The 107th Scout Troop, attached to Craiglockhart Church, marches on Princes Street, outside the North British & Mercantile building during a parade in 1948. *Courtesy of Hamish Davidson.*

❧ *Left.* This advertisement appeared in a souvenir edition of *The North British Station Hotel* (now the Balmoral) which was opened on 15 October 1902. Jenners, originally known as Kennington & Jenner, was opened at No. 47 Princes Street on Tuesday 1 May 1838, 'with every prevailing British and Parisian fashion, in silks, shawls, fancy dresses, ribbons, lace, hosiery and every description of linen, drapery and haberdashery'. Prior to 1838, Charles Jenner and Charles Kennington were employed by W. R. Spence & Co., silk mercers and linen drapers, of No. 21 Picardy Place, but they were dismissed for taking the day off, without permission, to visit the Musselburgh Races. Having no job, but a modicum of ambition, they decided to open their own rival business on Princes Street. The business was not an instant success but gradually they made progress and expanded on Princes Street and South St. David's Street. Charles Kennington retired in 1861 and died two years later, leaving the business in the sole charge of Charles Jenner. After Jenner died in 1881 he was succeeded by his partner, James Kennedy, whose descendants ran the business until 2005 when it became a House of Fraser store. *From 'The North British Station Hotel'.*

❧ *Below.* This 1950s view of Jenners, from high on the Scott Monument, shows the store bedecked, possibly for the coronation in 1953 or one of the Edinburgh International Festivals. When the picture was taken, Princes Street still retained the tramway system, central islands for passengers, and setts on the road surface. The mosaic, with the name 'Jenners' is visible at the entrance to the shop. *Photograph by Duncan McMillan.*

Right. The policeman on points duty is not overworked at the junction of South St Andrew Street and Princes Street. The corner building, at one time occupied by the Douglas Hotel, was demolished to make way for a much grander design, in 1906, by the architect, John J. Burnet for R. W. Forsyth, tailors and outfitters. The cable car on Princes Street has stopped to allow a passenger to board. *Courtesy of A. W. Brotchie.*

Below. George Washington Wilson's photographic series of Edinburgh and other parts of Scotland is almost unsurpassed for variety and detail. This 1860s view, looking east on Princes Street, shows the rather mundane collection of buildings on the site now occupied by the Balmoral Hotel. It was opened as the North British Hotel in 1902. *George Washington Wilson.*

Below right. This late-nineteenth century view, taken from the Scott Monument, shows an almost deserted Princes Street, but for a few carriages. The original stylish lamp standards at the front of what is now the Royal Scottish Academy are not yet impeding the passage of traffic. *Malcolm Cant Collection.*

❧ *Above left.* This 1940s view shows electric tram car 238, on service No. 24 to Comely Bank passing car 309 on service No. 14 to Granton. The tram on the left with the rounded roof was built at the Shrubhill works of the Corporation tramways in 1937. *Courtesy of A. W. Brotchie.*

❧ *Above.* The Scott Monument was designed by the relatively unknown architect, George Meikle Kemp, following a competition. The intended site was Charlotte Square but in 1840 work started on the site in East Princes Street Gardens. The foundations sit on rock about fifty feet below the level of Princes Street.
Malcolm Cant Collection.

❧ *Left.* Men and women in a well-ordered crowd at the east end of Princes Street wait their turn to board a rather odd assortment of cable cars, probably en route for Murray-field or Tynecastle. The main building behind the cars is the Palace Cinema, opened on Christmas Eve 1913. It closed in 1955 to accommodate an extension westwards by their neighbour, F. W. Woolworth, which closed in 1984.
Malcolm Cant Collection.

❧ *Above.* The Civic Exhibition was held at the Waverley Market from Monday 21 October to Saturday 9 November 1963. The site of the Waverley Market is now occupied by Princes Mall at the upper end of Waverley Bridge. The exhibition, entitled 'This is your City', was organised by Edinburgh Corporation to showcase the work of its various departments. The 71-page catalogue, with an introduction by the Rt. Hon. Duncan M. Weatherstone, Lord Provost of Edinburgh, included articles on the police, public health, education, parks, museums and libraries. The catalogue was fairly light on statistics but did mention that the Corporation's estimated expenditure for the city for 1963–64 was almost £16 million, of which just over £10 million was to be raised from the city's rating system, levied on the value of property. *Photograph by John K. Wilkie.*

❧ *Right.* The section on the city's museums included Huntly House (now the Museum of Edinburgh), Canongate Tolbooth (now the People's Museum), Lady Stair's House, Museum of Childhood and Lauriston Castle. The libraries consisted of the Central on George IV Bridge, seventeen branches, three mobile libraries and several hospital libraries. *Photograph by John K. Wilkie.*

❧ *Above.* This photograph is very similar to others that are known to have been taken, *c.* 1886, ten years after the Waverley open-air market was roofed over and laid out in a series of flower beds and ornamental ironwork. The picture gives considerable detail about the group of buildings on the site before the construction of the North British Hotel (now the Balmoral) in 1902. The building in line with the Nelson Column on Calton Hill is the original North British Station Hotel, with the offices of the East Coast Railway Companies and the Midland Railway on the ground floor. To the right of the hotel, the single storey building is Cook's Tourist Office offering a 'New Route to England'. Farther to the right is the rear view of several business premises on North Bridge: D. M. Dunlop, the hatter at No. 66; Scottish Property Investment Company at No. 62; and Liptons, the provision merchant at No. 59. *Malcolm Cant Collection.*

❧ *Left.* The same scene was dramatically altered by the construction of the North British Hotel in 1902 and R. W. Forsyth's department store in 1906. *Malcolm Cant Collection.*

On Wednesday 23 October 1861 the streets of Edinburgh were brought to a standstill by two major civic ceremonies: the laying of the foundation stone for the General Post Office in Waterloo Place; and, later in the day, a similar ceremony for what was then described as the Industrial Museum in Chambers Street. The illustration shows the grand preparations made at the site of the General Post Office where Prince Albert, the Prince Consort, laid the foundation stone. The jig, raised ready to assist the prince to lower the stone, can be seen at the north end of the canopied enclosure. After the ceremony, the royal entourage made its way up North Bridge to the university on South Bridge where it was met by the principal, Sir David Brewster, and members of the Senatus Academicus. According to the press reports of the time, the company then proceeded to the adjacent site of the museum 'through one of the windows of the University'.

❧ *Above*. The completed General Post Office building was very grand but it was not all built at the one time. It was erected on the site of the old Theatre Royal in Shakespeare Square, based on designs by the architect, Robert Matheson. Matheson's work is substantially the building seen in this photograph. By 1890 the building was found to be too small, as a result of which another architect, W. W. Robertson, was employed to double the south frontage. At the present day, this can best be seen from the east pavement of North Bridge. The building was extended yet again, further eastwards, in 1908, but it was not quite such a good match as different stone was used and the alignment had to be altered to avoid railway tracks at the Waverley Station. *Malcolm Cant Collection.*

❧ *Left*. Such a grand building also required a fairly substantial staff. Some of the postmen are photographed here outside the General Post Office, *c*. 1905. Prior to 1840, postal services in the United Kingdom were very expensive, but in that year Rowland Hill introduced the universal Penny Post. At the beginning of the twentieth century there were over twenty postal uplifts per day at some central post offices. *Malcolm Cant Collection.*

❧ Despite the presence of barriers, pedestrians appear to cross the junction at whatever point is convenient. The policeman on points duty is stepping out briskly, not to give himself exercise, but apparently to man both junctions at once. At certain times, the duty policeman was required to control traffic at the junction with North Bridge as well as at Leith Street and Waterloo Place. Rising serenely and timelessly above everthing is Robert Adam's beautifully proportioned Register House, begun in 1774, and built of stone from the quarries of Craigleith and Hailes. Its purpose, long delayed in implementation, was to house Scotland's public records. Internally, the grandest space is the rotunda, lined with shelves to hold the Register of Sasines. In 2008, the entire space was renovated as part of the ScotlandsPeople Centre.
Photograph by Norward Inglis.

PART 2

CHARLOTTE SQUARE

GEORGE STREET

ST ANDREW SQUARE

Part 2 includes Charlotte Square, George Street and St Andrew Square, all three being integral to James Craig's first plan for the New Town. Like Princes Street, George Street and the two squares were intended to be almost entirely residential. Each has developed very differently over the last two hundred years. Charlotte Square, although no longer entirely residential, is undoubtedly the most intact, especially the north side by Robert Adam. George Street, on the other hand, had some public or quasi-public buildings from an early date: the first Physicians' Hall, 1775; St Andrew's Church, 1782; and the Assembly Rooms, 1787. The Royal Society of Edinburgh building was slightly later, in 1843. There were also several commercial buildings, notably the banks and insurance companies: Clydesdale Bank, 1841; Commercial Bank of Scotland, 1843; Standard Life Assurance Company, 1897; Royal Insurance Company, 1898; and Commercial Union Insurance Company, 1908. George Street, as Edinburgh's business centre, held sway until the last decade or two when many of the commercial buildings began to be converted to pubs and restaurants. St Andrew Square has followed a similar trend with the demise of offices occupied by such heavyweights in the financial world as Prudential, Scottish Provident, Scottish Widows, Caledonian, Life Association, Eagle Star, Scottish Equitable, Norwich Union, Scottish Union and National and others.

Part 2 is again arranged topographically from west to east, beginning with Charlotte Square. Many of the photographs selected are from the 1950s, at a time when street parking was a very relaxed affair. Photographs of Edinburgh in the 1920s are not nearly so common as in other decades but a small group of interesting pictures taken in 1929 has been included. These are of Hope Street, South Charlotte Street and Charlotte Square lent to me some time ago by Malcolm Wood. Included is a photograph of the Hope Street office of George Hall, the cab and taxi hirer. The firm could trace its roots to the 1860s when they operated horse-drawn omnibuses. George Hall's fleet of 1920s Rolls Royces operated on the streets of Edinburgh until shortly after the end of the Second World War. Their stance was on the west side of Charlotte Square, where the cars faced out from the kerb. When a prospective customer phoned the office for a cab, George Hall took the details, strode out onto the pavement and gave a shrill blast on his whistle to summon the first available car. Not only that, but in the absence of irritating traffic management schemes, it drove the shortest route to the cab office. Another interesting firm whose history is briefly recorded is George Dobie, the George Street interior decorators, who were established in 1849 and are still operating at a different address in Edinburgh after one hundred and sixty years of service.

Edinburgh has a rich heritage of statues, sculpted by the most skilled craftsmen of their day, including Sir Francis Chantrey (1789–1841), Sir John Steell (1804–91) and John Rhind (1824–92). George Street has three statues at the intersections: George IV at Hanover Street (Chantrey); William Pitt, prime minister, at Frederick Street (Chantrey); and Thomas Chalmers, churchman, at Castle Street (Steell). The tradition has been maintained, at the present day, by Sandy Stoddart with his work, James Clerk Maxwell, the physicist, at the east end of George Street. Stoddart's other Edinburgh work includes: David Hume, philosopher, outside the High Court in the Lawnmarket; Adam Smith, economist, east of St Giles' Cathedral; and James Braidwood, firemaster, near the Mercat Cross. Other statues included in the New Town are perhaps less well known: the memorial to William Ewart Gladstone, prime minister, was moved from St Andrew Square to Coates Crescent gardens; and Emperor Alexander and his horse, Bucephalus, also at St Andrew Square was moved to the quadrangle of the City Chambers.

Several 1950s photographs by Norward Inglis have been included throughout the book. One of his most intriguing compositions has, however, created an enigma which may not yet have been solved. In his photograph of the George Hotel and St Andrew's Church in George Street he includes a long line of private cars parked nose-in to the pavement on the north side of the street. The cars generally are a cross-section of the motor car industry of the day – except for the last six which appear to share only two registration numbers!

This shop window display in George Street, probably James Gray & Son Ltd., ironmongers, included a model of a circus tent by Sandy Davidson to advertise Bertram Mills Circus, c. 1958. *Courtesy of Mrs Catherine Davidson.*

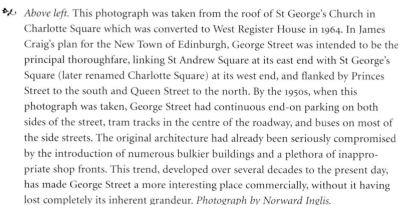

❧ *Above left.* This photograph was taken from the roof of St George's Church in Charlotte Square which was converted to West Register House in 1964. In James Craig's plan for the New Town of Edinburgh, George Street was intended to be the principal thoroughfare, linking St Andrew Square at its east end with St George's Square (later renamed Charlotte Square) at its west end, and flanked by Princes Street to the south and Queen Street to the north. By the 1950s, when this photograph was taken, George Street had continuous end-on parking on both sides of the street, tram tracks in the centre of the roadway, and buses on most of the side streets. The original architecture had already been seriously compromised by the introduction of numerous bulkier buildings and a plethora of inappropriate shop fronts. This trend, developed over several decades to the present day, has made George Street a more interesting place commercially, without it having lost completely its inherent grandeur. *Photograph by Norward Inglis.*

❧ *Above right.* Taken from the same vantage point, on the same day, the camera lens has been swung in a south-easterly direction, across the corner of Charlotte Square towards the Old Town, Salisbury Crags and Arthur's Seat. *Photograph by Norward Inglis.*

❧ *Right.* The Prince Albert statue, in the centre of Charlotte Square gardens, was unveiled by Queen Victoria on 17 August 1876. The waiting crowd of citizens and dignitaries was entertained by a choir and the band of the 79th Highlanders. The sculptor was John Steell who had already completed several other statues throughout the city. *Courtesy of Robin Sherman.*

Charlotte Square, designed by Robert Adam, was the last section of James Craig's First New Town to be built. Although ideas for developing the ground emerged about 1787, the square was not completed until 1820. The central garden was circular when first laid out in 1803 and was enlarged as an octagon in 1873. In Craig's drawings, the square was named St George's Square but this was changed to avoid confusion with George Square at Bristo. The photograph shows Robert Adam's north elevation which is considered to be one of his finest masterpieces. Bute House, at No. 5, is the official residence of Scotland's First Minister, and No. 7 is the Georgian House, opened to the public in 1975 by the National Trust for Scotland.

In this early 1950s photograph, parking around the square is very relaxed showing a good cross-section of the British car industry at the time: *left to right*: a Humber Super Snipe, 1949; a Standard Flying 8, 1946–48; a Wolseley 1938–39 or 1946–48; a Vauxhall 10 or 12hp, 1939 or 1946–48; and, on the extreme right, an Austin A70 Hampshire, 1948–50. *Photograph by Norward Inglis.*

The Northern Lighthouse Board was established in 1786 to cover Scotland, and, from 1815, the Isle of Man. At the present day, the board owns, operates and maintains 208 lighthouses around the coasts of Scotland and the Isle of Man. The first light to be established was Kinnaird Head, Fraserburgh, in 1787, and probably the most famous is the Bell Rock lighthouse, built in 1811, which is the longest standing rock lighthouse. For many years all lighthouses were manned but the first one to be automated was Fladda in 1956. The last Scottish lighthouse to be automated was Fair Isle South in 1998. Most of Scotland's lighthouses were designed and built by the Stevenson family of engineers, father and grandfather of Robert Louis Stevenson. The photograph shows the board's headquarters at No. 84 George Street.

The original St George's Church, in the centre of the west side of Charlotte Square, very effectively closes the vista looking west from George Street. The church was designed by Robert Reid, following Robert Adam's earlier design, but with much less detail. It was opened in 1814 at a cost of nearly £24,000 and was maintained without significant alteration for almost a century and a half. By 1960, however, there was evidence of serious dry rot, necessitating costly support work for the dome. St George's and St Andrew's, in George Street, formed a union on 7 June 1964, and left the problem of the building to the new owner. After the remedial work was completed in 1964 by the Ministry of Works, St George's Church became West Register House.
Both photographs by Norward Inglis.

Right. Hope Street, south of the photograph on page 31,

Above. The photograph shows the east side of South Charlotte Street in 1929. In a manner similar to Hope Street, the symmetry of the façade has been spoiled, this time by extending shop fronts out across the basement area. However, these have been put to good commercial advantage: No. 3 is Johnston, Green Ltd., fishmongers and poulterers, with a telegraph address 'Chicken'; and sharing the same street number, A. G. Spalding & Brothers (British) Ltd., athletic goods manufacturers, this time with the telegraph address, 'Golf'. On the corner of Princes Street, the premises with the wooden balustrade is occupied by John Sinclair, tobacco merchants, and Gerrard Bros., furriers. On the extreme left of the picture, the letters RAL, on the face of the building, is part of Clerical, Medical and General Life Assurance Company; and the projecting sign, on the extreme right, is for John Wilson & Son, Irish linen merchants. The road surface is laid with granite setts and there are no road signs or markings visible. The small car on the left is an Essex *c.* 1928, a low price version of the American Hudson. *Courtesy of Malcolm Wood.*

Hope Street, south of the photograph on page 31, included the large corner block at the junction with Queensferry Street. The building was occupied by: Aitken & Niven, clothiers for motoring coats and travelling wraps; Todd & Co., floral decorators; and George Hall, cab and taxi hirer. *Courtesy of Malcolm Wood.*

❧ *Above.* To the left of the lamp standard, the Roxburghe Hotel, with the light-coloured entrance porch, is on the east side of Charlotte Square, in 1929. Adjacent is the office of the Ocean, Accident & Guarantee Insurance Corporation Ltd., with the signage facing into George Street. The extensive ground floor, Nos. 142, 144 and 146, is occupied by James Wilson Ltd., butchers and poulterers, 'purveyors to His Majesty the King'. *Courtesy of Malcolm Wood.*

❧ *Left.* In 1937, George Street was the commercial centre of Edinburgh but retained a certain elegance and charm. The statues and the main buildings are extant. Farthest into the picture is the Melville monument in St Andrew Square, designed by William Burn and erected between 1820 and 1823. The tall steeple to the left is St Andrew's Church (St Andrew's and St George's from 1964), and at the junction with Hanover Street there is the statue of George IV, erected to mark the sovereign's visit to Edinburgh in 1822. The statue in the foreground is of William Pitt, prime minister from 1783 to 1801 and again from 1804 to 1806. Cabas, on the corner, were ladies' tailors.
Courtesy of Robin Sherman.

The junction of George Street and Castle Street is dominated by another of Edinburgh's famous statues. The image of Thomas Chalmers, sculpted by John Steell, stands on a high pedestal of red granite, erected in 1878. In silhouette, he appears to be looking down Castle Street to the statue of his fellow Disruptionist, Thomas Guthrie, with only a sideways glance towards the headquarters of the Church of Scotland. Any implied slight can only be coincidental, however, as the building, at No. 121, originally for the United Free Church of Scotland, was not erected until 1909, by which time the statue had been in place for more than thirty years. Thomas Chalmers was born in 1780 in Anstruther, the son of a general merchant and ship owner. In 1823 he became Professor of Moral Philosophy at St Andrew's University and in 1828, Professor of Divinity at Edinburgh. His greatest achievement was, however, as one of the leaders of the Disruption in 1843. Chalmers, Guthrie and almost five hundred ministers of the Church of Scotland marched out of the General Assembly and formed the Free Church of Scotland. They disagreed with an earlier Court of Session ruling which allowed a lay patron to choose a new parish minister, regardless of the wishes of the congregation. *Photograph by Norward Inglis.*

Norward Inglis took many photographs of Edinburgh but not many of them were 'night-shots'. The floodlit castle contrasts well with the shadowy darkness of an almost deserted Castle Street in the mid-1950s. On the left, at the junction with Rose Street, is the Resarus Co., which cleaned and pressed ladies' and gentlemen's clothes, and, on the other corner nearer to Princes Street, Charles Wilson & Son Ltd., butchers. Aitken Dott & Son, fine art dealers, are on the right. *Photograph by Norward Inglis.*

❧ *Top right.* George Dobie was born in 1824 to William and Agnes Dobie of Lanark. In 1849 after an Edinburgh apprenticeship, he started in business on his own as a painter and decorator at No. 15 Thistle Street. In 1866 he moved to grander premises at No. 23 George Street, photographed here in 1892.

❧ *Middle right.* The George Street premises extended to Rose Street Lane. There were two main salons, one to the front and the other to the rear that was used to receive customers. Between the two were the administrative offices. Equipment and stock were located near to the access from Rose Street Lane.

❧ *Bottom right.* In 1906, the firm bought No. 94 George Street but did not actually move in until 1912, the delay being partly caused by the amount of renovation work required. This 1921 photograph shows that a Citroen 7cwt. Farmer's Wagon had also replaced the horse-drawn, two-wheeled cart. *All photographs from* George Dobie Ltd., 1849–1949.

❧ *Above.* The new frontage was designed in 1929 in what was described as 'later Renaissance', affectionately referred to by the customers as the 'Old Curiosity Shop'. At the time of the centenary in 1949 the firm had been served by three generations of the Dobie family.

❧ *Above.* This undated view of George Street obviously belongs to a more leisurely age with a few carriages waiting at strategically placed stepping-on blocks at the kerbside. The photograph is taken looking east at the junction with Hanover Street. The statue of George IV is in the centre of the junction, erected after the king's visit to Edinburgh in 1822, and St Andrew's Church is in the centre of the picture. *Malcolm Cant Collection.*

❧ *Left.* When this photograph was taken of the interior of the Head Office of the Commercial Bank of Scotland in George Street, banking was a fairly sombre activity in which profits were announced in the annual balance sheet. The Commercial Bank of Scotland was founded in 1810 as the Commercial Banking Company of Scotland, and moved from the High Street to this new building on the south side of George Street in 1847. The building is now occupied as the Dome restaurant. *From 'The Story of the Bank of Scotland Ltd'.*

❧ A meeting of representative members of the Women's Voluntary Services was held on Thursday, 4 October 1951 at the headquarters of the Ministry of Works at No. 122 George Street. The purpose of the meeting was to decide what further action could be taken to improve the distribution of welfare foods to families in Scotland. Apparently the efficacy of the system was lagging behind other areas of the United Kingdom and the authorities had asked the WVS to assist. Any slight apprehension on the faces of some of the children might have been caused by knowing that the benefits on offer included cod liver oil and vitamin tablets. Some of the ladies, however, are full of admiration for Major C. R. Dudgeon, CBE, JP, who obviously had no difficulty in filling the role of Chief Food Officer for Scotland. Major Dudgeon was thanked for his encouraging address which was followed by loud applause, tea and biscuits. *Courtesy of Mrs Catherine Davidson whose mother-in-law, Mrs Jessie Davidson, is the lady on the extreme left of the picture.*

This mid-1950s photograph shows, on the left, the George Hotel, developed rather piecemeal from the original houses on the site that dated from the late eighteenth century. David Bryce made alterations in 1840, and MacGibbon & Ross in 1879. The next building is St Andrew's Church (later St Andrew's and St George's), designed by Andrew Fraser in 1782. The church was originally intended for St Andrew Square to match St George's in Charlotte Square. The five-storey building, on the right, was designed by W. Hamilton Beattie in 1898 for the Royal Insurance Company. At first sight there does not appear to be anything unusual about the cars parked obliquely to the pavement. However, closer inspection of the six motor cars to the left of the lamp standard reveals that five of them (perhaps six) share only two registration numbers. The car nearest to the lamp standard, registration number KLU 473 (London), is a Vauxhall Velox and the next car to the left, registration number SS 6930 (East Lothian), is a Humber Super Snipe. So are the others!

Photograph by Norward Inglis.

❧ *Above.* This very elaborate statue to William Ewart Gladstone, prime minister, is seen here at its original site at the junction of George Street and St Andrew Square. In 1955 it was moved to the gardens at Coates Crescent which had been its intended site in 1902. *Courtesy of Pat Scoular.*

❧ *Above right.* Continuing Edinburgh's grand tradition of erecting public statues and monuments is Sandy Stoddart's seated bronze of James Clerk Maxwell, the renowned philosopher, mathematician and physicist. The statue was erected at the east end of George Street in 2008. *Photograph by Phil Seale.*

❧ *Below right.* The Melville Monument and the Scott Monument have already been referred to earlier in the book. Catching the evening sun at the junction with George Street is the equestrian statue of Emperor Alexander and his horse Bucephalus. It was moved to its present site in the courtyard of the City Chambers to make way for the Gladstone statue. *Malcolm Cant Collection.*

❧ *Above left.* Below the monument to the Royal Scots Greys, peace and quiet is the order of the day in Princes Street Gardens. *Photograph by A. C. Robson.*

❧ *Above.* In the early 1960s, the 'onion' decorations on the south side of Princes Street augmented the 'butterfly wings' on the central lamp standards. *Photograph by A. C. Robson.*

❧ *Left.* Nearly half a century later, one of Edinburgh's leading floral attractions commemorates the Centenary of Scouting 1907–2007. *Photograph by Phil Seale.*

❧ *Above*. Darling's windows, at No. 124 Princes Street, during Christmas 1969, were dressed by their display manager, Yvonne Grant, and her team with a backdrop of Christmas wreaths on red lacquered doors against a white background.

❧ *Right*. Another of Yvonne Grant's designs appeared in Darling's windows in 1970. Abecita lingerie was shown to great advantage on the ground-breaking café au lait models.

❧ *Far right*. At Darling's in 1970, the display mannequin or model, Carmen, was a stunning first in a United Kingdom department store window. *All photographs by Campbell Harper. Courtesy of Yvonne Grant, display manager at Darling's from 1960 until 1971.*

❧ *Below and lower left.* During the Edinburgh International Festival of 1973, the windows of Small's at No. 106 Princes Street were also dressed by Yvonne Grant and her display team. The colourful tweeds and tartans were shown against a terracotta backdrop, with Edinburgh Castle depicted, in relief, by hundreds of minute silver mirrored pieces. *Photographs by A. G. Ingram. Courtesy of Yvonne Grant, display manager at Small's from 1971 until 1976.*

❧ *Bottom right.* Also at Small's, in 1975, the theme is 'The Spirit of Christmas': the centrepiece and gift boxes were created in Small's own display studio. *Photograph by Yvonne Grant.*

43

Edinburgh is fortunate to have such a wide variety of public clocks on memorials, churches, public buildings and shops.

❧ *Above left.* The War Memorial was erected at Haymarket by the Heart of Midlothian Football Club in memory of the players and members who fell in the First World War (1914–18) and the Second World War (1939–45). Photographed on 17 February 2006.

❧ *Above centre.* St Mary's Church in Bellevue Crescent dates from 1824. The clock was finished in 1826. Photographed on 1 September 2006.

❧ *Above right.* The clock-tower, with its lead belfry, forms part of Well Court built in 1883 in the Dean village. Photographed 3 November 2006.

❧ *Lower left.* The new West End clock, with its musical chimes, was erected on the corner of Binn's store (now Fraser's) in 1962. Photographed on 2 March 2006.

❧ *Lower centre.* The foundation stone for Register House was laid on 27 June 1774. The clock in the east tower was added in 1790. Photographed on 13 July 2006.

❧ *Lower right.* Ottakar's Bookstore in George Street took over the shop after the demise of Thin's which was established in Edinburgh in 1848. Photographed on 2 March 2006. *Photographs by Phil Seale.*

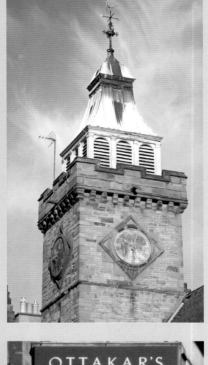

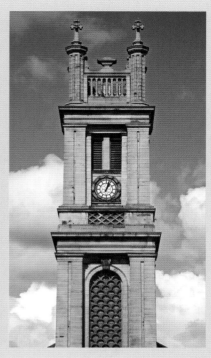

❧ *Above left.* The Balmoral Hotel was opened on 15 October 1902 as the North British Hotel, complete with enormous tower and clock faces. Photographed on 2 March 2006.

❧ *Above centre.* The Nelson Monument on Calton Hill was designed in 1807 by Robert Burn. It incorporated the time ball which rises and then falls in unison with the One O'Clock Gun at Edinburgh Castle. Photographed on 16 October 2006.

❧ *Above right.* St Stephen's Church in St Vincent Street was designed by William H. Playfair and built from 1827 to 1828. It is said that the clock had the longest pendulum in Europe. Photographed on 1 September 2006.

❧ *Lower left.* The clock-tower, clearly built out from a much plainer spire, adorned the building of the Edinburgh Savings Bank in Stockbridge. Photographed on 1 September 2006.

❧ *Lower centre.* St George's West in Shandwick Place was designed by David Bryce and built between 1866 and 1869 up to the clock stage. The campanile was added more than a decade later. Photographed on 28 April 2006.

❧ *Lower right.* Stockbridge Church (previously St Bernard's) in Saxe-Coburg Street was designed by James Milne in 1823. Photographed on 1 September 2006. *Photographs by Phil Seale.*

❧ *Above.* The Great Hall of the Royal College of Physicians Edinburgh at No. 9 Queen Street.

❧ *Right.* The Cullen Room at the Royal College of Physicians Edinburgh. *Courtesy of the Royal College of Physicians Edinburgh. Photographs by Phil Seale.*

Further information and photographs of the Royal College of Physicians appear on pages 62 and 63.

❧ The new interior of St Paul's and St George's Episcopal Church in York Place was designed by the architects, Lee Boyd. More information and photographs of St Paul's and St George's are on pages 72 and 73. *Photograph by Malcolm Innes. Courtesy of Lee Boyd Architects.*

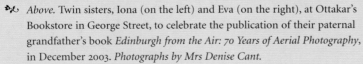 *Above.* Twin sisters, Iona (on the left) and Eva (on the right), at Ottakar's Bookstore in George Street, to celebrate the publication of their paternal grandfather's book *Edinburgh from the Air: 70 Years of Aerial Photography*, in December 2003. *Photographs by Mrs Denise Cant.*

PART 3

SHANDWICK PLACE

HAYMARKET

WESTERN NEW TOWN

QUEEN STREET

ST MARY'S ROMAN CATHOLIC CATHEDRAL

The Dean Bridge, designed by Scotland's foremost bridge builder, Thomas Telford, was opened in 1832. The building on the left is Kirkbrae House, parts of which date from the seventeenth century, and the church at the far end of the bridge is Holy Trinity, designed in 1838 by John Henderson. The car is a 1920s Rolls Royce. *Photograph by Norward Inglis.*

Part 3 begins at the West End and proceeds by Shandwick Place and Haymarket as far west as Donaldson's Hospital. It also covers significant parts of the western New Town and then turns eastwards, via Queen Street, to the area around St Mary's Roman Catholic Cathedral in Broughton Street.

Shandwick Place is shown, in 1937, at the height of the city's first electric tramway system. In recent months the street has suffered very badly from the preliminary roadworks required to enable the tracks to be laid for the new tram system. Trade has been badly affected, but will

return, although not quite with the same appearance as the photographs included of Mather's motor car showroom and Lipton's the family grocer.

Three main places of worship have been included to the west of the West End, appropriately, with origins covering different facets of the Christian faith: St George's West began as a Free Church; Palmerston Place Church finds its roots in the United Associate Secession Church; and St Mary's Cathedral in Palmerston Place is Episcopalian.

Haymarket was always, and will continue to

be, a transport hub. There are examples of cable cars, one of the first motor buses in Edinburgh, *c.* 1900, and a classic photograph of a horse tram, complete with four staff, about to begin its journey to Leith in 1890. Several streets in the western New Town are included, notably the very elegant crescents, Eglinton, Glencairn, Grosvenor and Landsdowne, as well as Wester Coates Avenue, St Andrew's Free Church in Drumsheugh Gardens (demolished for a classic 1950s blunder), and Melville Street and Crescent. Further north, Drummond Place and Heriot Row continue the theme of elegant crescents and terraces.

Queen Street was the northern boundary of James Craig's plan for the First New Town. A brief history of the Royal College of Physicians Edinburgh is included, from its humble beginnings in Fountain Court which ran from the High Street to the Cowgate. The physicians acquired a new home in 1775 in George Street, but, although it was a very grand building, they sold it, in 1843, to the Commercial Bank of Scotland and moved to their present home in Queen Street. There are photographs of the interior of the Queen Street building to augment those already seen in the colour section.

At the time of writing, the Scottish National Portrait Gallery in Queen Street is closed for extensive renovations, which means that Phil Seale's photographs are confined to the exterior of the building. However, it has given the opportunity to include pictures of several of the excellent statues which fill the niches on the face of the building.

The area around Picardy Place is the last location to be included in Part 3. St Mary's Roman Catholic Cathedral was built between 1812 and 1814, at a time when religious tensions were running high in Edinburgh. The cathedral has been altered and extended on numerous occasions to the point where only the façade is now original. The pedestrian area outside the cathedral is home to Eduardo Paolozzi's famous work, *The Manuscript of Monte Cassino*, which includes a gigantic foot, ankle and open hand, all in bronze.

On the last page, there are three illustrations relating to the Theatre Royal. The history of this ancient theatre has not been without its problems. The 'old' Theatre Royal, dating from 1768, was in Shakespeare Square on the site of the former General Post Office. When the theatre was closed in 1859 the name 'Theatre Royal' was transferred to an existing theatre in Broughton Street. Unfortunately, between 1859 and 1946 the theatre was burned down on no fewer than four occasions. Senior citizens of Edinburgh may recall that the shell of the last Theatre Royal stood for many years beside the cathedral until it was removed for an extension to Lewis's department store.

The roof 'garden' at Edinburgh Ladies' College, Queen Street, and the art room at the same school. *Malcolm Cant Collection.*

This 1937 view of Shandwick Place clearly shows private and public transport beginning to compete for the available road space. Tram rails from Princes Street and Hope Street converge, a few yards west of the West End clock where the policeman is on points duty. Shops on the left hand side of the road include: a milk bar; J. B. Watson, the optician; D. L. McGregor & Co., wine merchants; and John Downie Ltd., florists. Those on the other side of the road include: Lizars, the optician; George Cockburn, jeweller; and the Maypole Dairy Company. *Malcolm Cant Collection.*

Left. In the opening years of the twentieth century, Alexander Mather & Son of Orwell Terrace entered the new and challenging age of the motor car. They were agents for Clement's delivery vans and, in 1906, opened this car showroom at Nos. 79 & 81 Shandwick Place

Below left. Lipton's had shops at North Bridge and Earl Grey Street as well as their premises at No. 25 Shandwick Place. The right-hand window is entirely devoted to tea which was one of their main commodities.

Below. In 1906, when this photograph was taken, McAdam's Commercial Training Institution occupied extensive premises at Nos. 55 & 57 Shandwick Place. *All Malcolm Cant Collection.*

❧ *Above.* Shandwick Place, created from about 1806, absorbed Maitland Street in the late 1890s and Erskine Place in 1979. The most dominant building is St George's West Church, designed by David Bryce, begun in 1866, and opened on 24 October 1869. It was not until 1879 that the tower or campanile was completed to a different design by Rowand Anderson. At the Disruption in 1843, part of the congregation of St George's in Charlotte Square joined the Free Church with Dr Candlish. Initially, they worshipped at various locations until they had sufficient funds for the foundation stone of St George's West to be laid by the Earl of Dalhousie on 5 November 1867.

❧ *Right.* Palmerston Place Church was built between 1873 and 1875 to designs by the architects, Peddie & Kinnear. It is a very distinctive design of Italianate, pillared arcades flanked by twin, square stair towers with copper domes. The congregation was formed by the union of Palmerston Place Church and Lothian Road Church (now the Film House) on 2 May 1976. Previously, Palmerston Place Church had united with Belford Church on 5 April 1970. *Both Malcolm Cant Collection.*

🙢 *Above.* The Edinburgh Street Tramways Company ran these horse cars between Haymarket and Bernard Street. At the time it was a major part of Edinburgh's tram routes. The picture was taken *c.* 1890 at Clifton Terrace, Haymarket, where the horses were unyoked and led round to the other end of the car, ready for the return journey. To assist with identification, cars on each route were painted in different colours. On this route the main panels were red but other routes were white, yellow, blue or green. *Courtesy of A. W. Brotchie.*

🙢 *Left.* The photograph is taken at Haymarket, looking north into Grosvenor Street. The small vehicle in the centre of the picture is one of the first motor buses in Edinburgh, run by the Edinburgh Autocar Company between 19 May 1899 and mid-1901. The fare was one penny between Haymarket and the General Post Office at the east end of Princes Street. *Courtesy of A. W. Brotchie.*

The progress of this open-topped cable car in Haymarket Terrace is being greatly impeded by a slow-moving horse-drawn vehicle in front. Car 173 is on the route from Murrayfield to Nether Liberton, via Princes Street, and the advertisement is for Suchard's Cocoa. Edinburgh's new tramway system will avoid bottlenecks like Haymarket Terrace by being largely away from main thoroughfares between the airport and Haymarket.
Malcolm Cant Collection.

❧ *Above.* A class of young boys at Donaldson's, 1906, with David Scott fourth from the left in the back row. *Courtesy of Mrs Sheila Bell, daughter of David Scott.*

❧ *Left.* The magnificent quadrangle of Donaldson's Hospital at Wester Coates was designed by the architect, William H. Playfair. It was built of stone from Craigleith and Binny quarries by Young & Trench between 1842 and 1851. The photograph shows the hospital from the west with the original chapel projecting from the rear of the building. The hospital was founded after the death, in 1830, of James Donaldson, publisher and printer of West Bow, who left the sum of £210,000 'to build and found an hospital for boys and girls to be called Donaldson's Hospital preferring those of the name Donaldson and Marshall to be after the plan of the Orphan's Hospital in Edinburgh and John Watson's Hospital'. Pupils, many of whom had impaired hearing and speech, were first admitted on 16 October 1850. In 2008, Donaldson's School was relocated to a purpose-built school in Linlithgow. *Malcolm Cant Collection.*

❧ *Above left.* Eglinton Crescent, running between Palmerston Place and Magdala Crescent, was designed by John Chesser and constructed between 1875 and 1880. Its most distinctive external features are the grand doorways and bay windows at ground and first floor levels. The crescent was named after Susanna, Countess of Eglinton.

❧ *Below left.* Glencairn Crescent and Eglinton Crescent were built as a pair to enclose an elliptically-shaped private garden in the centre. The former was also designed by John Chesser and built from 1873, but the detail was not quite as good as that for Eglinton. Glencairn was named after Elizabeth, dowager Countess of Glencairn.

❧ *Above right.* Grosvenor Crescent forms a pair with Lansdowne Crescent, also enclosing an elliptical garden. It was designed by John Chesser but built slightly later than Lansdowne with much more elaborate detail. In the photograph the twin towers of St Mary's Cathedral have not yet been built.

❧ *Below right.* Lansdowne Crescent runs westwards from Palmerston Place from which it has an excellent view of the spires of St Mary's Episcopal Cathedral. The crescent was designed in 1865 by Robert Matheson, and named after the 3rd Marquess of Lansdowne.
All Malcolm Cant Collection.

❧ *Above left.* A solitary car stands outside the Grosvenor Hotel in Grosvenor Street. The street was designed in 1865 by Robert Matheson with parapets and dormers but the completed three-storey terrace turned out to be rather severe, with detail confined to the doorways only.

❧ *Below left.* The foundation stone for St Andrew's Free Church in Drumsheugh Gardens was laid in November 1884, and the building, designed by Campbell Douglas & Sellars and costing £18,000, was opened on 8 April 1886. The first sermon was preached by Dr Marcus Dods. The building was demolished shortly after the union, in 1955, with Clermiston Church Extension to form St Andrew's Clermiston.

❧ *Above right.* The delivery vehicle in Wester Coates Avenue belongs to Charles Wilson & Sons, butchers and poulterers, who had premises at No. 19 Castle Street (see page 35) and No. 298 Lawnmarket. Their telegraph address, long before the introduction of email, was 'Silverside'.

❧ *Below right.* A bronze statue of Robert Dundas, 2nd Viscount Melville, by Sir John Steell, was erected in 1857 in the centre of Melville Crescent. Melville Street, to the right, was designed in 1814 by Robert Brown with a very grand pillared centrepiece on the north side opposite Stafford Street. *All Malcolm Cant Collection.*

St. Mary's Cathedral, Edinburgh.

The entire western New Town is dominated by the spires of St Mary's Episcopal Cathedral in Palmerston Place. Before it was built, a temporary iron church was erected in 1876 under the charge of William Macdonald Meredith, which was closed when the cathedral was opened. St Mary's Cathedral was consecrated by Bishop Cotterill on 30 October 1879. It was financed by Mary and Barbara Walker, the last surviving grandchildren of George Walker, an Episcopalian minister who had been ordained in 1730 by James Dunbar, Bishop of Aberdeen. The Walker sisters left their entire fortune to the Episcopalian Church on condition that the money was used to build a cathedral on the site. The Gothic design by G. Gilbert Scott was eventually chosen and work began in May 1874. The west spires, not yet completed in the left-hand image, were not added until 1913–17. *Malcolm Cant Collection.*

❧ *Left.* Drummond Place forms a significant part of Edinburgh's northern New Town, planned by Robert Reid and William Sibbald in the first few years of the nineteenth century. This early 1950s photograph shows that the basic layout has survived more or less intact, and that even the stepping-on blocks, the railings and the granite setts in the roadway have been maintained. *Photograph by Norward Inglis.*

❧ *Below left.* Both of the main sections of Heriot Row, with their open outlook to Queen Street Gardens, were very popular, with most feus taken up by 1805. The section to the east of Howe Street, seen in this 2009 photograph, was designed by Robert Reid with two main storeys, rising to three at each end and in the centre. *Photograph by Phil Seale.*

❧ *Below.* The most famous house in Heriot Row is, of course, No. 17, the home of Robert Louis Stevenson from 1857 to 1880. Robert Lewis Balfour Stevenson was born in Edinburgh on 13 November 1850. His father was Thomas Stevenson of the famous family of lighthouse engineers and his mother was Margaret Balfour, daughter of the Rev. Lewis Balfour of Colinton Parish Church. *Photograph by Phil Seale.*

❧ *Above.* Sir Robert Sibbald, the eminent physician, is credited with being the founder of the Royal College of Physicians Edinburgh. He, and several colleagues, petitioned for a Royal Charter which was granted by Charles II in 1681. It was twenty-three years later, however, before the college secured anything like permanent accommodation. This was obtained on 1 December 1704, for 3,500 merks, to purchase rather run-down premises in Fountain Close, between the High Street and the Cowgate. *From 'Old Edinburgh' by James Drummond, 1853.*

❧ *Upper right.* By 1770, the poor state of the premises in Fountain Close was such that the college was required to find temporary accommodation at the Royal Infirmary. However, a site at the east end of George Street was secured and James Craig designed a new building in 1775. In 1843 the building was sold to the Commercial Bank of Scotland who demolished it to build their own headquarters, now occupied as the Dome restaurant. *From 'Modern Athens'.*

❧ *Lower right.* The college's next move was to their present home at No. 9 Queen Street, the foundation stone being laid by the president, Robert Renton, on 8 August 1844. The total cost of the building, designed by Thomas Hamilton, and also the furnishings, was £11,080. *Courtesy of the Royal College of Physicians Edinburgh.*

❦ *Left.* The Top Library at Queen Street was originally the College Museum which was fitted with display cabinets and free-standing show-cases down the centre of the room. The museum contained an extensive collection of materia medica which was transferred, in 1896, to the Pharmaceutical Society of Great Britain. *Courtesy of the Royal College of Physicians Edinburgh. Photograph by Phil Seale.*

❦ *Below left.* The New Library is entered either from the south-east corner of the Great Hall (see page 46) or from the curved corridor from the main staircase. The library, dating from 1876 by David Bryce, is based on the layout of the Bodleian Library at Oxford. *Courtesy of the Royal College of Physicians Edinburgh. Photograph by Phil Seale.*

❦ *Below.* Displayed on one of Bryce's tables in the New Library is the travelling medicine chest of Sir Stuart Threipland (1716–1805), president of the college from 1766 to 1770, who accompanied Prince Charles Edward Stuart during the 1745 Rebellion. Enclosed in this heavy mahogany box, ten inches square, are one hundred and sixty remedies and numerous miniature instruments. *Courtesy of the Royal College of Physicians Edinburgh.*

❧ *Above left.* John Campbell, 2nd Duke of Argyll (1678–1743), statesman and soldier: Hanoverian commander in the Jacobite rising of 1715. Sculpted by David Watson Stevenson and erected on the west façade in 1903.

❧ *Above centre.* The north-east tower has five statues, three of which are visible in this photograph. On the extreme left (seen in profile) is Sir Henry Raeburn (1756–1823), painter, sculpted by James Pittendrigh Macgillivray and erected in 1900. Facing slightly left is James Dalrymple, 1st Viscount Stair (1619–1695), lawyer, also sculpted by Macgillivray. Facing slightly right is John Napier of Merchiston (1550–1617), inventor of logarithms, sculpted by David Watson Stevenson and erected in 1898.

❧ *Above right.* John Knox (1505–1572), historian and reformer, sculpted by John Hutchison and erected on the west façade in 1902. *Information on the statues taken from 'Scottish National Portrait Gallery, A Portrait Gallery for Scotland', by Helen Smailes.*

❧ *Right.* The Scottish National Portrait Gallery on the south side of Queen Street was designed by the architect, Robert Rowand Anderson, and built from 1885 to 1890. Its Gothic style and red sandstone give it a striking appearance in an area of the New Town built predominantly of grey sandstone. It was financed by J. R. Findlay, the philanthropic owner of the *Scotsman* newspaper. On the north-facing façade the windows form continuous arcading at first floor level, interspersed with niches in which a wonderful array of statues repose.
All photographs by Phil Seale.

❧ *Left.* This gigantic bronze foot stands in the pedestrian area outside St Mary's Cathedral in Picardy Place. It is by Leith-born Eduardo Paolozzi (later knighted) and forms part of his famous work *The Manuscript of Monte Cassino.* The work also includes an ankle and an open hand which sit nearby. During 2009 it became clear that the entire work would probably require to be re-sited to allow construction work for Edinburgh's new tramway system.

❧ *Below left.* The Conan Doyle pub on the corner of York Place appropriately commemorates the Sherlock Holmes story.

❧ *Below.* The bronze statue of Sherlock Holmes was erected in Picardy Place and unveiled on 24 June 1991 by Professor Geoffrey D. Chisholm, then president of the Royal College of Surgeons, Edinburgh. It was donated to the City of Edinburgh by the Edinburgh and Lothians branch of the Federation of Master Builders on the occasion of their fiftieth anniversary. The statue is in memory of Sir Arthur Conan Doyle, creator of the legendary Sherlock Holmes. In July 2009, the statue was moved temporarily to allow construction work for the new tramway system.
All photographs by Phil Seale.

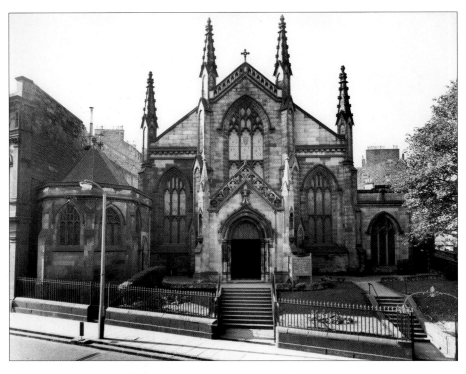

Right. The site of St Mary's Roman Catholic Church in Broughton Street was acquired in 1801 by Bishop Hay, using compensation which he had received for the wilful destruction of his earlier church in Chalmers Close at the top of Leith Street. The Broughton Street chapel, of which only the Gothic façade remains, was designed by James Gillespie Graham. Unfortunately, Bishop Hay died in 1811 but his successor, Bishop Cameron, began the building of St Mary's Chapel in 1812 which was opened in 1814. Over almost two centuries, the chapel was enlarged and altered on several occasions to the point where the present-day cathedral is an entirely different building (other than the façade) from the original chapel. The photograph was taken in the early 1960s. *Photograph by John K. Wilkie.*

Below. The staff of St Mary's Cathedral, 1905. *From left to right, back row*: Fr. Long; Fr. Couttenier. *Front row*: Fr. Logue; Canon Stuart (Administrator); Fr. Macdonald. *Courtesy of the Administrator of St Mary's Cathedral.*

Below right. The Red Mass is held to mark the opening of the Law Court session. *From left to right*: J. J. Maguire, advocate (later Sheriff Principal); David Brand QC (later Lord Brand, High Court and Court of Session judge); Lord Wheatley; and Lord Carmont. *Courtesy of the Administrator of St Mary's Cathedral.*

❧ *Above left.* The congregation of St Mary's Roman Catholic Cathedral praying for President John F. Kennedy in 1963. Known as *JFK*, he was the thirty-fifth president of the United States (1961–63), the first Roman Catholic to hold the post, and the youngest man ever to be president.

❧ *Below left.* Mrs Jane Gray (née Oddy), mother of Cardinal Gray, knitting by her fire with her cat by her side.

❧ *Above right.* The choir of St Mary's, in 1959, conducted by the director of music, Arthur Oldham, who was later the conductor of the Edinburgh Festival Chorus.

❧ *Below right.* In 1939 the cathedral had a thriving boxing club. *Left to right, standing*: P. Nicol; J. Hughes; Fr. Gallacher; D. Sutherland; Mr Blaney. *Sitting*: F. Nolan; I. Connelly; F. Sweeney; J. Dignan; G. Twiss. *All photographs courtesy of the Administrator of St Mary's Cathedral.*

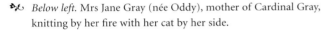

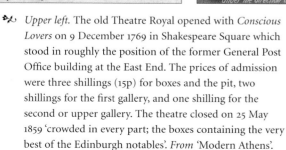

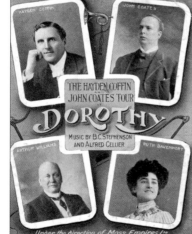

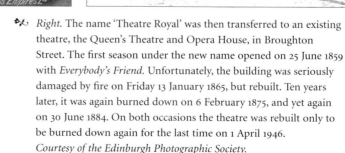

🌺 *Upper left.* The old Theatre Royal opened with *Conscious Lovers* on 9 December 1769 in Shakespeare Square which stood in roughly the position of the former General Post Office building at the East End. The prices of admission were three shillings (15p) for boxes and the pit, two shillings for the first gallery, and one shilling for the second or upper gallery. The theatre closed on 25 May 1859 'crowded in every part; the boxes containing the very best of the Edinburgh notables'. *From 'Modern Athens'.*

🌺 *Right.* The name 'Theatre Royal' was then transferred to an existing theatre, the Queen's Theatre and Opera House, in Broughton Street. The first season under the new name opened on 25 June 1859 with *Everybody's Friend.* Unfortunately, the building was seriously damaged by fire on Friday 13 January 1865, but rebuilt. Ten years later, it was again burned down on 6 February 1875, and yet again on 30 June 1884. On both occasions the theatre was rebuilt only to be burned down again for the last time on 1 April 1946. *Courtesy of the Edinburgh Photographic Society.*

🌺 *Lower left.* Moss Empires Ltd. advertised a wide variety of entertainment at the Theatre Royal including the very popular comic opera, *Dorothy.* *Malcolm Cant Collection.*

PART 4

YORK PLACE

BROUGHTON

BELLEVUE

CANONMILLS

STOCKBRIDGE

HILLSIDE

CALTON

Part 4 deals with the areas of the New Town to the north and east. It begins at York Place and proceeds northwards, via Broughton and Bellevue, to Canonmills and Stockbridge. This section concludes with several pictures of Hillside and Calton.

St Paul's and St George's Episcopal Church has stood on the corner of York Place and Broughton Street since 1818, but it has not stood still – especially in the last few years. The original church cost £12,000 to build and was extended eastwards (towards Broughton Street) by the

addition of two bays in 1891. Other alterations and improvement have been done over the years, but none so ambitious as the complete redesign and refurbishment of the interior by the architects, Lee Boyd, completed in 2008 at a total cost of £6.8 million, or approximately five hundred and sixty-six times the cost of the original church. Any reservations that there may have been about the plans must surely have been addressed by seeing the completed work, shown on page 47 of the colour section. St George's Church united with St Paul's in 1932. Much of the exterior of St George's Church in York Place still exists but is rather inappropriately masked by a 1934 warehouse and showroom used in recent years for bathroom and kitchen fittings.

The area around Broughton Place and Hart Street has produced some interesting photographs of vehicles used by the Church Army, F. A. Scott, the local motor contractor, and a young beau in his recently acquired 1919 Ford, model T.

Further north, the area around Bellevue has been devoted to the various churches, two of which have been lost. The beautiful Gothic steeple of St Mary's Free Church on the corner of Albany Street and Broughton Street was demolished and replaced with an office building, and St Bernard's Davidson Church in Eyre Place ended its days as a confectionery warehouse before being replaced by flats. At least two very good church buildings remain, however, the

This young man, Frank, is obviously very proud of his greatly modified 1919 Ford, model T, with a left-hand drive. The spare wheel and the accessory petrol can are mounted on the running board. The photograph was taken on 7 January 1924 in Broughton Place. *Malcolm Cant Collection.*

Catholic Apostolic Church and St Mary's in Bellevue Crescent.

Stockbridge has always been considered as Edinburgh's New Town 'village'. It is not nearly as ancient as Corstorphine, Colinton or Duddingston, but over its comparatively short lifetime it has been home to several of Scotland's foremost painters: Henry Raeburn, David Roberts and Robert Scott Lauder. Photographs of Stockbridge include Church Street, Saunders Street and India Street being demolished, Raeburn Place, and David Macaskill outside his family grocer's business in St Stephen Place.

The areas of Hillside and Calton are taken last. The selection begins with a panoramic view *c.* 1867 looking north from Calton Hill. Unlike any of the other pictures in the book, the opportunity has been taken to include a numbered inset guide showing the position of the main buildings. Although many of the shops and tenement buildings in Leith Walk have not yet been built, the general topography is not greatly different from the present day. We then return briefly to the East End and follow Waterloo Place and Regent Road. In view of the proximity of Holyrood Palace, both Regent Road and Waterloo Place have featured in many royal processions over the years as they made their way past the former Royal High School and St Andrew's House.

The last photograph in the book is a 1930s aerial view of Calton Hill. It includes all the main buildings and monuments which have contributed to the idea of Edinburgh being the Athens of the North. Included are the National Monument, the Nelson Column, the City Observatory and other memorials. From the historian's point of view, however, the most interesting part of the picture is the inclusion of the demolition site of Calton Jail and the Bridewell. All of the main part of the jail has been removed and the Bridewell has had its perimeter wall and gatehouse taken down.

The garage on the east side of Pitt Street (later renamed Dundas Street) was designed in the Art Deco style by the architects, Reid & Forbes, in 1931 for John Player & Sons, coach and motor hirers. In 1946 Player sub-let part of the premises to Electrobat who were factors and repairers of Exide batteries. Alexanders of Edinburgh occupied the garage between 1954 and 1979. The car parked outside is an Austin 16, *c.* 1932. *Courtesy of Douglas Glass.*

🎝 *Above left*. St Paul's Episcopalian Chapel (now St Paul's and St George's Church) on the north side of York Place, was designed by Archibald Elliot, built by Thomas Beattie of Leith, and completed in 1818 at a cost of £12,000. The illustration shows the original building of seven bays only, with octagonal towers and innumerable Gothic spires along the roof line. *From* 'Modern Athens'.

🎝 *Below left*. This photograph shows the interior of the church as it was in 1958. As part of the work done in 1891 by Kinnear & Peddie, the original aisle galleries were removed to create a much more spacious interior. The stained glass at the west end consists of ten lights which were moved from the east end when the church was lengthened. *From* The Story of St Paul's and St George's Church.

🎝 *Above right*. In this second view, the church building has been skilfully extended by an additional two bays to the east. This was done under the direction of Kinnear & Peddie, architects, in 1891–92. The work entailed taking down most of the east gable, including two turrets, and rebuilding to include a new sanctuary. *From* The Story of St Paul's and St George's Church.

🎝 *Below right*. St George's can trace its roots back to 1708 at Half Moon Close. In 1722 the congregation moved to Blackfriars Wynd, then in 1774 to a new chapel in the Cowgate, and finally to York Place in 1793. In 1932 the congregations of St Paul's and St George's united. The photograph shows the rear of the former St George's building in York Place in 2009. *Photograph by Phil Seale*.

Left. In 2008 St Paul's and St George's reopened after extensive remodelling of the interior by the architects, Lee Boyd. The total cost, which included a large extension to the rear to include various meeting rooms, was £6.8 million, most of which was raised by the congregation. Side balconies were reintroduced which increased the church's capacity from four hundred to nearly eight hundred. A glass pavilion was also built at the west door to provide a sheltered, welcoming entrance off York Place.

Below left. In order to facilitate the extensive building programme, the congregation moved out in January 2006 and worshipped at Pollock Halls, as well as holding other services at The Hub in the Lawnmarket. At the end of August 2008 a week of special celebrations was held to mark the reopening of the church, including two thanksgiving services on Saturday 30 August.

Below. The ornamental rood screen, dividing the chancel from the nave, was replaced shortly before the 2008 remodelling of the interior of the church. *All photographs courtesy of St Paul's and St George's Episcopal Church.*

❧ *Right.* There is plenty of action in this work station created by the Church Army to produce logs and sticks for Edinburgh's many coal fires. In the Edinburgh Church Army Report for 1934 there is mention of labour and lodging homes and a stick factory for men at Nos. 24, 26 and 28 Broughton Place. The men were under no special restrictions 'but must conduct themselves in an orderly manner while residing in the Home'. Beds were available for one shilling (5p) per night. There was also a boarding house for women at No. 12 Hart Street and a women's dining room at No. 9 Cowgate.

❧ *Below.* This 1924 Ford, at the junction of Hart Street and Broughton Place, was owned by F. A. Scott, motor contractor, of No. 19 Hart Street. *All Malcolm Cant Collection.*

❧ *Below right.* One of the delivery vehicles was a Morris Commercial, *c.* 1925, photographed at the foot of Hart Street in May 1927. All safety precautions have been taken: the dog is standing guard; and the rear wheel has an added brake in the form of a wooden wedge. In the course of 1934, the total value of the firewood produced and sold was £2,031. The delivery vehicles were also used to bring in, to a central collecting point, donations of clothes, boots and books.

Broughton Place, Edinburgh.

Left. Broughton Place was feued from 1807. The north side (left) was built as a long elegant terrace of two-storey houses rising to three storeys at each end and at the pedimented centrepiece which can be seen in this 1910 view. At the far end of the street is the pillared portico of the former Broughton Place Church, built in 1820, but lacking its intended tower and spire. Broughton Place Church and McDonald Road Church united on 2 May 1974.

Below left. This 1911 view is of the east side of Scotland Street, looking north to the buildings and advertising boards at Scotland Street Goods Station. Scotland Street began in 1823 as Caledonia Street. The street trader is Peter Victory, fish merchant, who had his shop at No. 230 Leith Walk.

Below. Barony Street runs west from Broughton Street. It takes its name from the ancient Barony of Broughton, parts of the village surviving well into the twentieth century. The two-storey building on the right, near the horse and cart, is the Glasite Meeting House now the home of the Architectural Heritage Society of Scotland.
All Malcolm Cant Collection.

❧ *Above left*. The Catholic Apostolic Church is the substantial building on the left of the picture. It was probably designed by John Dick Peddie and built *c*. 1843. At the present day it is renowned for the preservation of the Phoebe Traquair murals. The spire of St Mary's Free Church can be seen on the skyline.

❧ *Below left*. St Mary's Free Church was erected in 1862 on the corner of Albany Street and Broughton Street at a cost of £13,000. It was designed in the French Gothic style by J. F. Rocheid with a grand tower one hundred and eighty feet high. St Mary's Free Church became St Mary's United Free Church in 1900 and Barony in 1929.

❧ *Above right*. The angle from which this photograph has been taken, *c*. 1911, appears to accentuate the fact that the tower and spire of the church in Eyre Place were never completed. The church was designed by John Starforth and built between 1879 and 1881. Eyre Place Church became Davidson United Free in 1900, Davidson in 1929 and St Bernard's Davidson in 1945.

❧ *Below right*. St Mary's in Bellevue Crescent takes centre stage in Bellevue Crescent. It was designed by Thomas Brown, City Superintendent of Works, and built for the city as a Burgh church. It cost £13,000 and was opened on 12 December 1824. *All Malcolm Cant Collection.*

❧ *Left.* The photograph, *c.* 1904, in Pitt Street (renamed Dundas Street) shows a cable car on the first Edinburgh route from Goldenacre to Hanover Street. It is a few hundred yards south of the junction with Henderson Row (on the left) where the power station was erected to drive the underground cables in perpetual motion, that is, until they broke down. The car was originally owned by the Edinburgh Northern Tramways Co., Ltd., but, by the time this photograph was taken, it belonged to the Edinburgh & District Tramways Co., Ltd. In the background are the old gas works at Tanfield where the Standard Life Assurance Company later built one of their main offices. *Courtesy of A. W. Brotchie.*

❧ *Below left.* The electrified former cable car No. 218 is heading south on Brandon Terrace, about to start the steep climb up Pitt Street to Princes Street, up the Mound, and along Lauriston Place to Tollcross. Assuming that the car is on service No. 23, it would then go via Bruntsfield to Morningside Road Station. The present-day clock in the centre of the junction at Canonmills was not erected until 1947. The small car in the left-hand corner of the picture is a Humber 10, *c.* 1920. *Courtesy of A. W. Brotchie.*

❧ *Above.* The photograph was also taken in Brandon Terrace – only about a year before the demise of Edinburgh's first electric tramway in 1956. It shows service No. 23 to Morningside Station. *Photograph by George Staddon.*

Right. The view is north down Church Street in Stockbridge immediately before the demolition of the old properties in India Street on the left. Church Street was formed along the line of what was Kirk Loan, a very early route between Stockbridge and St Cuthbert's Church at the West End of Edinburgh. Church Street was renamed Gloucester Street in the mid-1960s. The building on the right of the picture, with the mansard roof and numerous advertisements on the gable end, is Duncan's Land where David Roberts, the artist, was born and had his studio. The building has a lintel stone, FEAR GOD ONLYE 1605 I R, which was moved to Stockbridge from houses which were taken down in the Lawnmarket to allow the opening up of Bank Street at the top of the Mound.

Below. Church Place, nearby, also provided ideal opportunities for advertisements: Hudson's Soap, fine powder for the people; and Lyon's Tea.

Below right. When the old tenements of Saunders Street were being demolished it does not appear that the area was adequately fenced off, which created a wonderful, but dangerous playground for the local children. *All photographs by John K. Wilkie.*

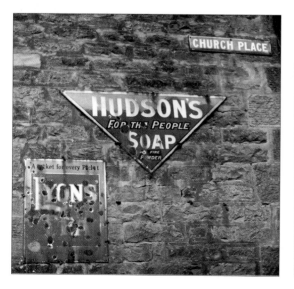

Deanhaugh Street, Edinburgh.

❧ *Above left*. This undated photograph shows the junction of St Bernard's Row, on the left, and Raeburn Place, leading onto Deanhaugh Street where the cable car is. The clock-tower of the former Edinburgh Savings Bank can just be seen in the distance. *Courtesy of Robin Sherman.*

❧ *Below left*. Mr Donald Macaskill ran his grocer and wine merchant's shop from No. 2 St Stephen Place from 1943 until his retirement in 1970. The photograph was taken about 1948. Before buying the business in Stockbridge from the previous elderly owner, John A. Smith, Mr Macaskill had been manager of various branches of the well-known grocery chain of the day, Cooper & Co. During the years of the Second World War, and for several years thereafter, the public were required to register with a local grocer to ensure that they received, in exchange for cash and coupons, their entitlement to basic provisions, usually referred to as 'rations'. *Courtesy of Iain Macaskill.*

❧ *Above*. St Stephen's Church was built between 1827 and 1828 for £18,975 to designs by William H. Playfair. It was a most difficult site to develop as the natural contours of the ground fell away steeply to the north. This resulted in Playfair designing the main doorway, at the top of the steps, to enter the building at gallery level, an arrangement which was eventually altered in the 1950s to create the main body of the church at gallery level. *Malcolm Cant Collection.*

This panoramic view, looking north from Calton Hill, is dated *c.* 1867. Names are quoted as they were in 1867. *Malcolm Cant Collection.*

1. Pillared gable at Blenheim Place, designed in 1821.
2. Leopold Place, designed 1820.
3. Montgomery Street was started in about 1823 but later plans were interrupted by the North British Railway (see 9 below).
4. Clapperton, Oliver & Co., cabinetmakers, showroom at Nos. 59 & 60 Princes Street.
5. Royal Terrace, begun in 1821.
6. Windsor Street, begun in 1823.
7. Pilrig Free Church, designed by Peddie & Kinnear, 1861.
8. Leith Walk.
9. Goods station for the North British Railway almost ready for opening on 2 March 1868.
10. Continuation of Leopold Place.
11. Greenside Church, opened on 6 October 1839.
12. Hillside Crescent, begun in 1825 and continued in 1880.

Left. Regent Terrace, looking west, in the early 1950s, presents a very unified façade, greatly enhanced by the trellis balconies at first floor level and Doric columns on each side of the doorways. Norward Inglis, the photographer, whose work is reproduced throughout this book, lived and worked at No. 18. *Photograph by Norward Inglis.*

Lower left. This 1905 view, taken from Leith Walk, looks east along London Road, with the rounded, pillared corner into Elm Row on the left, and Royal Terrace and Greenside Church on the right. *Malcolm Cant Collection.*

Below. Greenside Church was designed by James Gillespie Graham and built from 1831, but the square tower with battlements and pinnacles was not completed until 1852. It was opened for worship on 6 October 1839. The present Greenside congregation was formed on 22 January 1978 by a union with Hillside. *Photograph by Norward Inglis.*

Right. Car No. 50 on service No. 14 is about to turn down Leith Street, *c.* 1955. The car, normally used on service No. 6, the Marchmont Circle, had non-standard seats that could be rotated when the car was being prepared at the terminus for the return journey. Standard seats had backs which could be flipped over to face in the opposite direction.
Courtesy of A. W. Brotchie.

Below. Pedestrians cross at Waterloo Place in the gathering gloom, 1950.
Photograph by Duncan McMillan.

Below right. The Scottish Rest Home for Servicemen was at No. 20 Waterloo Place during the Second World War. The serviceman who wrote this post card said that he had just met his old pal, Jim, in Princesse (*sic*) Street and that he did not know when they would finish their babeling (*sic*).
Malcolm Cant Collection.

❧ *Left.* The photograph, dated May 1910, is taken as the royal entourage passed the Calton Jail in Regent Road. The picture is not sufficiently clear to identify the occupants of the carriage but George V acceded to the throne on 6 May 1910 and was crowned at Westminster Abbey on 22 June 1911. The foundation stone for Calton Jail was laid in September 1815 and the building was ready two years later to receive internees from the Canongate Tolbooth. St Andrew's House was built on the site of the Calton Jail and adjacent Bridewell from 1936 to 1939. *Malcolm Cant Collection.*

❧ *Below left.* A large crowd has gathered in Regent Road outside St Andrew's House on 24 June 1953 for the ceremonial drive which took place in Edinburgh to mark the Coronation of Queen Elizabeth II at Westminster on 2 June. The State Drive began at St Giles' Cathedral, proceeded down the Royal Mile to Holyrood Palace, up Regent Road, along Waterloo Place into Princes Street, and up the Mound, back to St Giles'. The parade was headed by a detachment of the Scots Guards. *Photograph by Norward Inglis.*

❧ *Below.* During the same Coronation visit, the Queen and the Duke of Edinburgh are driven down Regent Road, accompanied by the Household Cavalry, guarded by the military, and watched by a passing liege. *Photograph by Norward Inglis.*

Right. According to *The Royal High School*, by William C. A. Ross, the school can trace its origins to the opening years of the sixteenth century. Since then it has been in several locations including St Mary's Wynd, Friars Wynd, Kirk o' Field, Blackfriars, High School Yards, Calton Hill and lastly, Barnton. The most commanding building is, of course, the Grecian temple on Regent Road, designed by the architect, Thomas Hamilton, and built from 1825 to 1829. After the school moved to East Barnton Avenue, the Regent Road building was adapted for use by an intended Scottish Assembly which failed the referendum in 1978. Sadly, at the present day, this magnificent building is not being fully utilised, but not for want of imaginative suggestions, not all of them worthy of the building.
Malcolm Cant Collection.

Below. Gas lighting on the approach pathway from Waterloo Place to Calton Hill was picturesque but not really adequate in 1950. *Photograph by Duncan McMillan.*

Below right. Several generations of boys will recall that the library at the Royal High School remained relatively unaltered, except for an occasional change of furniture. *Courtesy of Iain Macaskill.*

In this aerial photograph of 1930 the cleared site of Calton Jail can be seen on the extreme right. Beside it, and only partially demolished, is the Bridewell. The foundation stone for the Bridewell, Edinburgh's 'House of Correction' designed by Robert Adam, was laid by the Earl of Morton on 30 November 1791. Both the Bridewell and Calton Jail were demolished for the construction of St Andrew's House. By contrast, the principal monuments on Calton Hill remain largely unaltered. Only twelve pillars were erected of the National Monument to those who fell in the Napoleonic Wars. The intended copy of the Parthenon by C. R. Cockerell and William H. Playfair would have greatly enhanced the city's claim to be the Athens of the North. To the right of the National Monument, the Nelson Column was designed in 1807 by Robert Burn. The square enclosure, almost in the centre of the picture, contains: the cross-shaped City Observatory, 1818; Observatory House, 1776 on the south-west corner of the boundary wall; and the square monument to Professor John Playfair on the south-east corner, designed by his nephew, the architect, William H. Playfair. Outside the enclosure, on the right, is the monument to the great philosopher, Dugald Stewart, and, further down Regent Road, a similar circular colonnade to Robert Burns. *Malcolm Cant Collection.*